Mae's Night Flight

Fran Baird Innes

Illustrated by Stanimir Stoilov

Tuckamore Books
a CREATIVE PUBLISHERS imprint
St. John's, Newfoundland
1993

© 1993, Fran Baird Innes

Appreciation is expressed to *The Canada Council* for publication assistance.

The publisher acknowledges the financial contribution of the *Department of Tourism and Culture, Government of Newfoundland and Labrador,* which has helped make this publication possible.

All rights reserved. No part of this work covered by the copyrights hereon may be reproduced or used in any form or by any means—graphic, electronic or mechanical—without the prior written permission of the publisher. Any requests for photocopying, recording, taping or information storage and retrieval systems of any part of this book shall be directed in writing to the Canadian Reprography Collective, 214 King Street West, Suite 312, Toronto, Ontario M5H 2S6.

The author wishes to thank:
  The Newfoundland Writers Guild for helpful criticism and encouragement;
  Nora Lester for editorial comment;
  Tim Wynne-Jones for setting me on the right course.

∝ Printed on acid-free paper

Illustrated by Stanimir Stoilov

Published by
Tuckamore Books
an imprint of CREATIVE PUBLISHERS
A Division of Robinson-Blackmore Printing & Publishing Ltd.
P.O. Box 8660, St. John's, Newfoundland A1B 3T7

Printed in Canada by:
ROBINSON-BLACKMORE PRINTING & PUBLISHING LTD.
P.O. Box 8660, St. John's, Newfoundland A1B 3T7

Canadian Cataloguing in Publication Data

  Innes, Fran Baird
    Mae's night flight
    ISBN 1-895387-29-9

I. Stoilov, Stanimir. II. Title.

PS8567.N63M33 1993   jC813'.54   C93-098657-1
PZ7.I66Ma 1993

To my beloved granddaughter
Emily Avis Innes
in celebration of her
first birthday

Boom...Boom.
She dived under the covers.

Ra...Oom.
She put her hands over her ears and the noise disappeared. As soon as she took her hands away, **Boom**, the thunder began again. It was giving her a tummy ache. She curled into a ball, pulled the pillow over her head and pressed it against her ears. "I'm a big girl now" she said to herself over and over again until she felt all warm and cosy, and very sleepy.

Boom... Cr.rack... Boom

... went the thunder. Mae pushed the pillow away and looked out from under the blanket. A flash of lightning lit up the window and thunder crashed and rumbled overhead. It was no use, she couldn't get back to sleep with all that noise.

"I am Thor, mighty god of thunder! How dare you tell me what to do." As the rest of the bird-man appeared, he reached for a cloud and hurled a torrent of rain right at Mae. It clattered against the window.

"You big bully," Mae shouted, "You stop making all that noise, don't you know what time it is?"

"*Time ... Time*, what's Time got to do with it?" Thor looked puzzled as he waved his arm and drew out another knife of lightning.

Mae ducked as it streaked past her window. "Time has a lot to do with it. It's time I got some sleep, that's what! Besides, your old thunder and lightning really scares little kids."

"Oh really?" said Thor. "are you ... what's your name?"

"Mae" she said.

"Mae! Well then Mae, tell me, are you scared of thunder?"

"Well, I am scared but I am angry too. I need my sleep tonight, because tomorrow is the very most important day of my life."

"Huh! Tomorrow is only when the sun decides to come up and take a look around. What's so special about that?"

"Well, it may not be special to you up there, throwing your old lightning around and making all that thunder and keeping people awake and scaring me half to death, but..."

Boom...Crack...Boom.

Mae covered her eyes as the sky exploded.

"You big bully, you stop that, do you hear!"

"No, you stop, missy" Thor bellowed. "Nobody calls me names and it is I, Thor, who gives the orders here."

When Mae didn't reply, he swooped past her window. She stood quite still with her eyes shut and her hands over her ears.

He threw heavy raindrops against the window until Mae opened her eyes.

"That's better." said Thor, "I really didn't mean to scare you but you made me mad too. After all, I was up here, minding my own thunder and lightning business, when you butted in. Why don't you come on up and see how I manage things. That might help."

Thor reached out his hand and Mae, expecting another torrent of rain, dropped the curtain. This time nothing happened.

When she looked out the window again, Thor beckoned to her to come on up.

"But I don't know how to fly" she called.

"Spread your arms and think light and leave the rest to me."

Mae looked to the right, then to the left. She watched the faint flashes of lightning and listened to the **Ra . . . oom** of distant thunder as Thor pushed it further and further away.

"I'm master here," the Thunder God boasted, "You have nothing to fear, come on up and I'll show you around."

Cautiously, Mae opened the window and breathed in the cool night air. Then, spreading her arms and imagining herself as light as thistledown, away she flew. Thor floated towards her.

"Come on, just follow me. It's easy once you get the hang of it!"

Mae, a little wobbly at first, followed Thor up through a path of lightning, high into the heavens. In no time at all she could turn east or west, north or south, through the night sky. She soared clear over the top of Cabot Tower and headed for the harbour, but a black thunder cloud hid it from her view.

"I don't suppose, Thor, you could get rid of that cloud down there," she called over her shoulder. "I did want to show you the lights..."

"No trouble," Thor replied. "Just watch me!" and pulling out a lightning knife, he hurled it towards the harbour. The knife carved a large hole through the middle of the dark cloud.

"Now see how I make thunder."

Mae watched as Thor pointed his hands at the black hole and made big circling motions. Both halves of the cloud began to spin towards the hole.

Before Mae could say **"WOW,"** they crashed into each other.

Boom...Boom...Boom

went the thunder. Away the clouds flew, right up over the South Side Hills. Red, yellow, blue, green and white lights twinkled all around the Harbour. It was even more beautiful than Mae remembered from last summer, when her parents had taken her up Signal Hill to see the city at night.

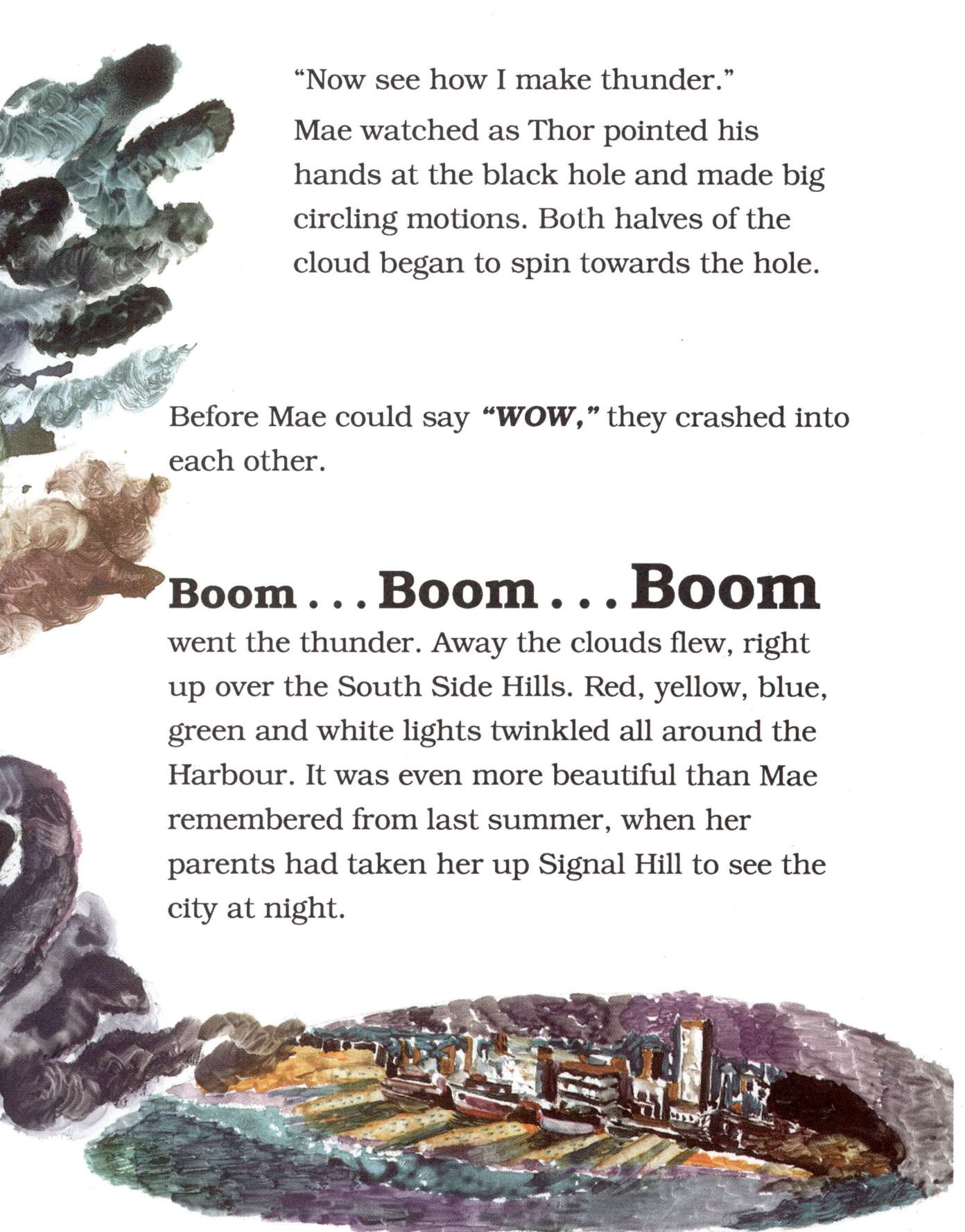

"Wow" she said. "This must be the most beautiful place in the whole wide world!"

"The whole wide world is pretty beautiful Mae, and your harbour is a very special place. But come along, we have lots more to see."

This time, Mae flew ahead. She hithered and thithered, this way and that, down Signal Hill, out through the Narrows and over the ocean, which shimmered in the moonlight.

As they climbed towards the moon, she looked back in time to see a pod of humpback whales romping in the sea. She waved to them and they spouted water from their blow-holes in greeting.

They flew with the wind, through the mist and along the milky way. Mae was having such a good time she wanted to reach the little dipper and use it to catch the raindrops which still fell from the distant clouds.

She could have flown on forever but Thor led her towards a small crack of light in the eastern sky. The crack grew wider and wider and finally it pushed the night right over the edge of the earth.

"By the way," Thor said as he guided her down through the misty dawn "You haven't told me why today is the most important day of your life."

"Goodness, I nearly forgot! Today is my first day of school. Now don't you think that's pretty important?"

"Indeed it is, and we had better get a move on. It wouldn't do for you to be late. Come on, we're nearly there."

As they swooped down, they were joined by
a flock of starlings chattering and calling,
searching the distant horizon
for signs of ripe, red berries.

Down,
down they flew
until Mae's feet touched
the ground. The starlings
settled in the dogberry tree,
right in her own front yard!
The grass, wet from the rain,
squished through her toes as she
ran toward her front door.

All that flying about had made her very, very sleepy.

When Mae awoke, she lay still as a mouse. She listened for the Boom of thunder but didn't hear a sound.

Throwing the covers off her head, she looked toward the window expecting to see a flash of lightning. All she saw was the sun streaming into the room.

Quickly hopping out of bed, she ran to look out the window. The sky, as blue as her new corduroy overalls, was dotted with marshmallow clouds all soft at the edges from the heat of the sun.

Mae felt absolutely great!

She opened the window and looked high up in the sky. "Good-bye Thor" she called as loud as she could.

Then she ran out of her room, down the hall and right into her parents' bedroom. She climbed into the big bed between her mother and father.

Her mother gave her a hug. "We expected you last night when it thundered."

"Yes, weren't you scared? It was a doozy of a storm, you must have heard it," Her father rumpled her hair.

"Oh yes I heard it all right," Mae answered with a secret smile.